Garden
in the Snowy
Mountains

GARDEN IN THE SNOWY MOUNTAINS

AN INNER JOURNEY WITH CHRIST AS YOUR GUIDE

Christopher Biffle

1817

Harper & Row, Publishers, San Francisco

New York, Grand Rapids, Philadelphia, St. Louis
London, Singapore, Sydney, Tokyo, Toronto

FIRST EDITION

Library of Congress Cataloging-in-Publication Data

Biffle, Christopher.
    Garden in the snowy mountains : an inner journey with Christ as your guide / Christopher Biffle. — 1st ed.
        p.   cm.

    ISBN 0-06-060789-0 (pbk.)
    1. Spiritual life.   2. Jesus Christ—Miscellanea.   I. Title.
BV4501.2.B485   1989
248.4—dc20   89-47185
                                                                        CIP

89 90 91 92 93 KRUEG 10 9 8 7 6 5 4 3 2 1

To my beloved daughter Persephone,

"Of her choice virtues only gods should speak
Or English poets who grew up on Greek
(I'd have them sing in chorus cheek to cheek)."

THEODORE ROETHKE

Contents

"Yet the Lord pleads with you still: Ask where the good road is, the godly paths you used to walk in, in the days of long ago. Travel there, and you will find rest for your souls . . . "

JEREMIAH 6:16

Introduction

THIS is a book to help you see your relationship with Christ more clearly. On the following journey, in the form of a long spiritual dream, you will explore your past and see the places where God has touched your life. You will clarify the major aspects of your relationship with him now. And you will find ways to grow closer to God in the future.

In almost every chapter you will speak, face to face, with Jesus. All you will need is a pen.

The Bible provides ample precedent for God's speaking through dreams. By thoughtfully filling in the blanks ahead, you will make this dream your own. You will discover the difference between the old self that keeps you from God and the new self that cleaves to him.

Read slowly in a quiet place. Put on your favorite meditative music if that will help your reflections. Because this is a slender book, you might be tempted to finish it too quickly. I recommend you work through not much more than a chapter a day.

On the dream journey that is about to begin, you seek wisdom about God. Expect to find wonders.

CHAPTER 1

The Journey Begins

ONE night lying in bed, you hear an inner voice, only partly your own, ask, "Are you ready to seek God?"

"Yes," you whisper. You close your eyes for a few long moments and open them in a snowstorm.

You are trudging through a wintry wood on a dark afternoon.

Small limbs on the black trees all around creak as they move up and down in the wind. Over your head the limbs are like a tangle of snakes against the darkening sky. Leaning forward into the wind, you follow an icy road of hoofprints and cart tracks through the hard snow.

You carry a Bible.

The road is higher in the center and you walk there out of the ruts of frozen mud. Each time the road bends, the wind cuts against your face. You arrive at a small clearing. Pale wild grasses stick up stiffly through the snow. The wind makes your eyes water.

The road curves across the frozen clearing toward a tumble of hewn timbers and a sheltering wall. You walk in the torn pennants of steam your breathing makes.

Crossing the snowy clearing, you look up at the winter's sky. The gray clouds rise up in stormy mountains.

Once across the clearing you stand out of the wind with your back against the frozen turf wall of a collapsed hut. The road dissolves here. There is no gap in the dark wall of trees surrounding the clearing to show a direction. You crouch down inside the small heat your body makes.

A blackbird rises out of a bare tree into the wind and is blown back, cawing, to its perch.

Crouching makes nothing but a minor nest of pains. The wind twirls three yellow leaves across the frozen snow. You believe you are at the center of nowhere.

You must move. Which way?

Having no idea, you open the Bible. The cold wind turns the pages and stops at the story of the prodigal son. You read the first verses.

And he said, "There was a man who had two sons; and the younger of them said to his father, 'Father, give me the share of property that falls to me.' And he divided his living between them. Not many days later, the younger son gathered all he had and took his journey into a far country, and there he squandered his property in loose living." (Luke 15:11–13)

Looking around the snowy clearing you say to yourself, "This is a dream . . . but I can remember my life before this dream began! I was like the prodigal son. Some of the gifts God gave me that I wasted

were _____

_____

_____."

With a cold finger, you slowly trace the words in the Bible.

"And when he had spent everything, a great famine arose in that country, and he began to be in want. So he went and joined himself to one of the citizens of that country, who sent him into his fields to feed swine. And he would gladly have fed on the pods that the swine ate; and no one gave him anything. But when he came to himself he said, 'How many of my father's hired servants have bread enough and to spare, but I perish here with hunger! I will arise and go to my father, and I will say to him, "Father, I have sinned against heaven and before you; I am no longer worthy to be called your son; treat me as one of your hired servants." ' " (Luke 15:14–19)

You whisper into the cold wind, "Before this dream journey, what were my sins?" And you answer, "Some of them were _____

_____

_____."

You continue reading the parable of the prodigal son:

"And he arose and came to his father. But while he was yet at a distance, his father saw him and had compassion, and ran and embraced him and kissed him." (Luke 15:20)

Thinking about the father embracing the son you feel _____

_____.

"And the son said to him, 'Father, I have sinned against heaven and before you; I am no longer worthy to be called your son.' But the father said to his servants, 'Bring quickly the best robe, and put it on him; and put a ring on his hand, and shoes on his feet; and bring the fatted calf and kill it, and let us eat and make merry; for this my son was dead, and is alive again; he was lost, and is found.' " (Luke 15:21–24)

You look at the wall of trees around the snowy meadow and the dark mountains of clouds above them.
"I must think more deeply," you say wisely, "In what parts of my past was I most like the prodigal son? The truth is _____

_____

_____

_____

_____."

You see Christ.
He walks toward you from the dark wall of trees.

Your heart knows it is the Holy One.
Rising, you face him.
"Follow me," he says.

You reply, "_____

_____

_____."

CHAPTER 2

The Dark Wood

You walk beside Jesus across the snowy clearing and feel _____

_____.

You look at his face and see _____

_____.

"Do not be afraid," he says, and his voice sounds _____

_____.

You reply, as you both enter the dark wood, "Lord, _____

_____

_____."

"We have far to go but I will not leave your side," he says lovingly.

Hearing this, you feel _____.

In the cold and darkness of the trees, you remember one of the most difficult times of your life.

Unable to keep silent, you say, "Lord, the darkness of this wood

reminds me of when _____

_____

_____

_____."

    "Did you seek me then?" he asks gently.

    "_____," you reply, and realize _____

_____.

    You walk behind Jesus through the dark wood for a long time and cannot help remembering other difficult events in your life. You recall when _____

_____

and when _____

_____.

Looking up at a bare oak you cannot tell where the treetop ends and the dark sky begins. You remember a painful time when _____

_____.

Ahead, through an opening in the black trees you see the cold winter moon and know a long night is beginning.

    You think about the darker aspects of your present life and see a person who _____

_____

_____.

You think about the darkest possibilities of your future life and see a person who might become _____

_____

_____.

    You want to unburden your heart to Jesus. You want to talk to him about the darkest parts of your past and the pain that still remains. You want to talk about the problems you face in your present life. You need to talk to him about your fears and doubts about the future.

And so you begin, "Lord, I remember when . . . "

Talking to Jesus about
Your Past, Present, and Future

_____

_____

_____

_____

_____

_____

_____

_____

_____

_____

_____

_____

_____

_____

_____

_____

_____

_____

_____

_____

_____

CHAPTER 3

At the Center of the Night

WHEN you have finished speaking, Jesus turns to you, and in the wintry darkness asks, "Who do you say I am?"

You answer him, "_____

_____."

Ahead on the path you see three dark Shapes. You can hear, but cannot see, the tree limbs as they creak in the strong wind overhead. The three Shapes move toward you through the dark hall of trees.

Wisely drawing closer to Jesus, you feel _____

_____.

The three Shapes wear robes the color of storm clouds.
The first Shape says, "I am Night, the time of error."
The second Shape says, "I am Winter, the season of death."
The third Shape holds a black orb as dark as the darkness between the stars and says, "I am Fear. Winter and Night are my vassals."
They all speak in the same whispering voice only slightly louder than the wind.
Jesus waits to see what you will say.

You respond truthfully, "I am one who _____

_____

_____

_____."

Night wears a silver ring shaped like the waning moon and asks, "What do you seek?"

And you reply, "I seek _____

_____."

"Perhaps that," says the Night, "is what you once had and now have lost."

You believe this means _____

_____

_____.

Winter holds a branch of yellow leaves and asks, "Who are you when you are lost from God?"

You answer, "When I am lost from God I am one who _____

_____

_____."

"Then that," says Winter, "is what you forget and now remember."

You believe this means _____

_____

_____.

Fear holds the black orb in both hands and simply asks, "Why are you afraid to love more deeply?"

You answer Fear, "_____

_____

_____

_____."

"We bring you three visions," Fear says.

You look toward the dark world of trees. There, within a cloud of light, is an aged figure.

CHAPTER 4

The First Vision

T HE shadows of the trees spray backward from the bright shell of
the vision.

You see a stooped figure with a deeply carved face, holding
the stump of a candle in one thin hand, and your heart knows
it is you on the last day of your life.

The figure's eyes are _____ and the
face is _____. You turn to Jesus
and he says lovingly, "These visions bring you wisdom about your
future, past, and present."

Looking at the vision of yourself near death, you realize _____

_____

_____

and feel _____.

The aged figure moves painfully toward you and says, "You have

many days left to you. Give me my life to live over and I would __

_____

_____."

CHAPTER 5

The Second Vision

LIKE a cloud slowly changing its shape in a storm, the vision changes.

You see a second image of yourself.

A child, partly light and partly flesh, stands against the dark wall of trees. Your heart pounds as you stare at yourself.

Turning to Jesus, you say, "This is an image of me when I was

about _____years old." The child's eyes are _____

and the child's face is _____.

You ask the vision, "Why are you here?"

The child answers in a voice you recognize, "To bring you wisdom. You have changed. I would never have believed you would become someone who _____

_____

_____."

CHAPTER 6

The Third Vision

L IKE light moving in water, the vision changes.

The child becomes a figure standing in black chains. You recognize the face. Your heart knows it is a vision of your present self.

The vision says, "What you do that cripples your spiritual

life is _____

_____

_____."

As the vision vanishes you turn to Jesus and say, "Lord, _____

_____

_____."

Night, Winter, and Fear pass beside you. You feel a feather's stroke of cold wind brush your cheek.

Far off, a rooster crows.

CHAPTER 7

The Cloudy Dawn

FOLLOWING Jesus through the dark wood and up a long, rocky hill, you think back over the experiences on your journey thus far and say to yourself, "The things I need to remember are ___

_____

_____

_____

_____."

You emerge from the wood and the air is warmer. Far to the east the sky is light gray. Below you, in the faint light of dawn, you see a broad frozen lake with five islands.

Jesus opens the Bible for you and in the dim first light you read:

If I speak in the tongues of men and of angels, but have not love, I am a noisy gong or a clanging cymbal. And if I have prophetic powers, and understand all mysteries and all knowledge, and if I have all faith, so as to remove mountains, but have not love, I am nothing. (1 Cor. 13:1–2)

Jesus asks you, "If you did nothing but follow love, what would you do with your life?"

You pause for a few moments and then say, "Lord, I would stop

_____

and I would start _____

_____.

I would continue _____

_____

_____. My goals would

change from _____

_____

to _____

_____."

CHAPTER 8

The Frozen Lake

THE sky in the east is filled with gray petals of light.

You stand with Jesus outside the dark walls of trees on the brow of a hill above the silvery lake.

"This is the Lake of the Heart," he gently says to you.

The five islands are dark against the silver lake. A blackbird is blown across the sky. Jesus puts his hand upon your shoulder and

you feel _____

_____.

You see the five islands form a cross.

CHAPTER 9

The First Duke

LOOKING into Christ's eyes, you see _____

_____

and feel _____

_____

and know _____

_____.

Then you look back at the frozen lake.

You are facing east toward the dawn. Three islands form the long vertical bar of the cross, and one island to the north and one to the south form the shorter horizontal bar.

Walking down the hill with Jesus toward the island at the foot of the cross, you wonder what will happen on your journey across the

Lake of the Heart. You hope _____

_____.

You step out through the weedy borders of the lake onto the ice. The lake is frozen the same gray as the sky. Walking with Jesus, you feel as safe as if the ice were granite.

The island ahead is covered with dark, bare oaks.

From the island's black shore, a horseman comes pounding toward you.

You step closer to Jesus. The horse comes thrashing onward in a dry mist of snow. The rider is dressed all in yellow.

Turning toward him, you make your face grin. He wheels up before you, the horse stamping and twisting at its bright bridle, and for moments you stand with the rider in the same freezing cloud of snow. You feel as if he has galloped to you from somewhere out of the sky or under the earth.

His armor is yellow as marigolds; his visor is the color of new butter; the silk trappings on his horse are bright as fool's gold.

The yellow rider announces, "I am one of the Merry Dukes of Disorder! We delight in waylaying foolish travellers!"

"I am _____," you say, "and I delight in

_____

_____." You try to speak boldly.

You turn toward Jesus but can tell he does not choose to speak. The rider seems afraid to look at him.

"I am Hardness of Heart," says the Yellow Duke. "What do you seek?"

"Wisdom about God," you answer wisely.

"Who do you need to forgive?" the Yellow Duke demands as he jerks back cruelly on the horse's bright bridle.

"No one," you say too quickly.

He laughs until he gasps for breath and, wiping merry tears from his eyes, he says, "If you are seeking wisdom, then you are certainly seeking the right thing!"

He laughs again and the explosive sound is like a big spoon beating on a metal wash pan.

You need to make some answer. You say, "Well, _____

_____."

He does not hear. The Yellow Duke yanks his horse about and races up the hill toward the black ramparts of the wood. Horse and rider merge in the distance into a single golden animal.

"Who do you need to forgive?" Jesus asks you quietly.

Thinking back over your life, you can do nothing but say to him

slowly and honestly," _____

_____

_____."

"What is most difficult for you to forgive?"

Standing in the dawn light from the east, you say to him, "____

_____

_____."

"What does God forgive you for?" he asks you lovingly.

You remember when you thought about your sins while you read the parable of the prodigal son. Now you want to describe them more completely.

"Lord, the people I have sinned most grievously against are ____

_____

_____

_____. And

my worst sins are _____

_____."

"Love the people you are bitter toward as I love you," Jesus says, looking into your eyes.

You answer, "Lord, _____

_____

_____," and you realize _____
_____.

    Then, as you continue walking with him toward the base of the cross of islands, you talk to him about people you need to forgive. "Lord," you begin, "I remember when . . ."

A Talk with Jesus
about People You Need to Forgive

_____

_____

_____

_____

_____

_____

_____

_____

_____

_____

_____

_____

_____

_____

_____

_____

CHAPTER 10

The Fortress of Oaks

WHEN you have finished talking to Jesus, he says kindly to you, "Repent of your sins and seek the kingdom of heaven."

You answer Jesus, "_____

_____

_____," and looking at his face you know

_____

_____.

In the eastern sky you can now see two snowy peaks with a feathery wall of bright clouds behind them.

You follow Jesus into the broad shadow of the first island. Ahead on the shore of the island is a dark archway.

Jesus says, explaining the journey ahead, "This is the Arch of Thorns. We will visit this island and the three other outer islands in the lake and return here by night. In the morning we will go to the island at the center of the cross. Today until noon, we will think about your past. From noon until twilight, we will think about your present. And tomorrow, on the island at the center of the cross, you will see your future."

Looking up into the dome of the sky where it is still night, you see a white crown of stars.

"Lord, more than anything on the journey ahead, I wish _____

_____

_____."

You stand beside Jesus at the Arch of Thorns. The arch is a massive, weathered trellis for two huge, dead rosebushes. The bushes twine about the pillars on your right and left and meet in a knotty mass of thorns above your head.

Beneath the knotted mat of branches you can see strange, large letters carved across the top of the arch.

"The words are in Hebrew," Jesus says. "They say, 'All is vanity,' says the Preacher!"

He stands close beside you and asks, "What do they mean to you?"

You answer him, "_____

_____

_____."

The branches are thicker than your forearm and the path through the arch is so clogged with black thorns that you are not sure you will be able to find a way through.

You try to follow Jesus, but though he passes through easily, the thorns tear at your skin and pull you back. You think of one of the greatest trials in your life. Struggling through the maze of brambles, you remember you believed you might never be happy again. It was

when _____

_____

_____.

Even now, as you pull free from a springy wand of thorns, you still

feel the old pain. You remember _____

_____

_____.

When you are beside Jesus, at last, he says, "For the gate is narrow and the way is hard, that leads to life, and those who find it are few" (Matt. 7:14).

You answer him, "_____

_____

_____."

Jesus guides you onto the island and stops in an icy clearing. In the middle of the clearing is a wide square of heavy oaks growing so closely together that you could not put your hand between the trunks.

Twenty huge oaks stand on the side facing you. There are rosy shards of the dawn sky in their highest branches.

Jesus walks around the wall of oaks to the left and you follow him.

On the second side of the square, a heavy wooden gate stands between two trees and is crowned with a span of interlacing limbs.

A huge, white, thornless rose is painted on the gate. Across the top of the gateway are carved Hebrew words.

"The words say, 'I had heard of thee by the hearing of the ear, but now my eye sees thee' " Jesus says quietly (Job 42:5).

He stands by your shoulder in the pink dawn light and asks, "What do they mean to you?"

You answer him, "Lord, I heard of you and now I understand

_____

_____."

Jesus opens the gate for you. Nothing is inside the Fortress of Oaks but snow.

You walk inside and notice the sky is light enough to give you a ghostly shadow. Jesus stands at the gate and watches. You walk around within the square of trees and feel you are looking for something, but there is nowhere to look.

At your foot, almost invisible among the ice crystals, is a snowy Pearl.

You look to see if there are more, but it is the only one.

Holding it in your palm, staring at it in the pink first light, the

Pearl reminds you of _____

_____.

The Pearl reflects and holds the whole world around you. It is a small globe with its own snow and pink light and dawn clouds.

A blackbird swoops down and plucks it from your palm.

CHAPTER 11

Memories of Love

THE blackbird flies off above the tops of the oaks with a grain of light in its beak.

At Jesus' side, you say to him, "Lord, right now I _____

_____

_____."

He answers you, "The kingdom of heaven is like a merchant in search of fine pearls, who, on finding one pearl of great value, went and sold all that he had and bought it" (Matt. 13:45–46).

You can still feel the place in your hand where the Pearl rested.

You say to Jesus, "Lord, the kingdom of heaven to me is _____

_____

_____."

You follow Jesus through the dawn light off the island and onto the silvery frozen lake.

Just as when you were in the dark wood you could not keep from thinking about painful times in your life, now, holding the memory of the Pearl in your hand, you cannot keep from thinking about love.

Walking behind Jesus toward the second island, you remember a

close time between you and _____,

a very important person in your life. What happened was _____

_____

_____.

You remember more close times with this special person and others. Walking in Jesus' shadow, you remember when _____

_____

_____

_____.

And when _____

_____

_____.

Far back in your past you remember loving times when _____

_____

_____

_____

_____.

And so, as you make your way through the morning toward the distant isle, you seriously begin the exploration of your past. You talk to Jesus about your memories of love and the special people who brought love into your life.

"Lord, some of my first memories of love were when . . ."

Talking to Jesus
about Memories of Love

_____

_____

_____

_____

_____

_____

_____

_____

_____

_____

_____

_____

_____

_____

_____

Talking to Jesus
about Memories of Love

_____

_____

_____

_____

_____

_____

_____

_____

_____

_____

_____

_____

_____

_____

_____

_____

_____

_____

CHAPTER 12

Two Problems

W HEN you have finished talking to Jesus about your memories of love, he turns to you and says, "Love God with your whole heart, mind, and soul, and love your neighbor as yourself."

The coppery winter sun hangs between the two snowy peaks on the eastern horizon. Far ahead, a giant black tree grows out of the frozen lake.

You say sadly to him, "Lord, what keeps me from loving God

more completely is _____

_____. What keeps me from loving others

exactly as you wish is _____

_____."

Jesus takes your hand for a moment and you feel _____

_____

_____.

CHAPTER 13

The Second Duke

TROTTING toward you across the silvered lake is a horseman all in green.

The plume on his helmet is green as clover, his armor is emerald green, and merry green ribbons are tied in his beard. He pulls his horse to a halt and stares down at you.

"I am False Values, one of the Merry Dukes of Disorder," he announces in a jolly way. You see a bracelet of wild grasses woven around his wrist.

"I am _____, one of those who

_____

_____," you answer him.

Jesus does not speak and the Green Duke will not look at him.

"I bring you a riddle about your past life, traveller," the Green Duke says chuckling. "What were your valueless valuables?"

You reply, "I am not sure what you mean, but I guess my answer

would be _____."

Before you finish speaking, the Green Duke is laughing. His laughter is harsh as stones rattling into a bucket. He spins his horse about and, still laughing, rides away.

Jesus explains, "He was asking you what you valued that had no value."

"I am not sure I understand, Lord."
"What have you given too much importance to?"

"Lord, the truth is _____
_____
_____."

"Which activities have taken you farthest away from me?"

You answer truthfully, "_____
_____
_____."

"What have you spent too much time thinking about?"

You say to Jesus, "_____
_____
_____."

"Then those are your valueless valuables."

"What I should have done, Lord, was to _____
_____
_____."

Ahead you see the sky-filling black tree.

CHAPTER 14

The Black Tree

STANDING at the base of the great tree, you feel like a child. The black tree seems large enough to hold a storm in its branches.

Hanging from the lower limb is an iridescent cloak.

"Look what I have found," you say to Jesus, and you pull the bright cloak over your shoulders. It has all the colors of a peacock's tail.

Jesus does not answer you.

Climbing over the black roots of the tree with the cloak tight around your shoulders, you crouch down and announce, "I want to rest here."

Stroking the brilliant cloak with the back of your hand, you think about other precious possessions.

As a child the things you wanted more than anything else were

_____

_____

_____

_____.

Looking up into the sky-filling tree, you remember other things you wanted as you grew older. You remember _____

_____

_____

_____.

Still later in life, you would have given anything to own a _____

_____

_____.

    The black branches above your head seem to fill heaven.

    Recently, the thing you lusted to buy for yourself was a _____

_____because _____

_____.

"Oh!" you think, "life would be perfect if I just had enough money

to _____."

    Jesus says, "This is the cloak of covetousness mentioned by Peter in his letter to the Thessalonians," and pulls the gaudy thing from your shoulders.

    "Lord," you confess, "the possessions that took me farthest from

your spirit in the past were _____

_____."

    "You cannot serve the world and God at the same time."

    "Lord, the things I do that serve the world and not you are ___

_____

_____

_____

_____."

CHAPTER 15

The Island of Memories

A red drape of clouds hangs between the distant snowy peaks. You follow Jesus across the frozen lake toward the second island and think about him.

When you think about his life, what impresses you most is

_____

_____

_____.

Of everything he did, you wish you could have been there when

_____

_____

_____because _____

_____

_____.

Looking at him as he strides ahead of you right now, you feel

_____

_____

_____.

Ahead on the second island you see two white stone towers with a bridge between them. The tower on the left is windowless; the tower on the right has many steepled windows and bright banners hanging from its battlements.

Looking at Jesus walking in a cloud of snowy light reflected from the lake, you ask yourself a wise question, "What must I do to be more like him?"

And you whisper, "I must start _____

_____.

I must stop _____

_____.

And I must continue _____

_____."

The island is sandy. You are close enough to see the banners hanging in the morning light on the tower on the right. The first banner is as dark blue as deep water, the second banner is green as spring wheat, and the third is red as the heart's blood. On each is emblazoned a white rose as tall and broad as an angel standing with wings outspread.

"This is the Island of the Past," Jesus says as you follow him toward the towers. "On the left is the Tower of Healing and on the right is the Tower of Blessings."

"What must I do, Lord?"

"Inside the Tower of Healing are three landings. As we climb the stairs, strong and sometimes painful memories will come back to you. Seek wisdom."

Jesus opens the heavy iron gate at the base of the Tower of Healing and you follow him inside to the bottom of a winding staircase. On the right side of the staircase is a painting in a gold frame with a large, glittering ruby set in each corner. On the left side is a painting in a battered wood frame with a tarnished copper coin set in each corner.

Jesus takes a flaming torch from the wall and you are amazed to see both paintings are images from your childhood.

Looking at the gold-framed painting you see one of the happiest

scenes from your childhood. You see _____

_____

_____.

Looking at the wood-framed painting you see one of the most painful

images from your childhood. You see _____

_____

_____.

Beneath this painting is one of your broken toys. It is _____

_____.

You feel _____

_____. You want to speak to Jesus but, as at many times in your life, you foolishly keep silent.

Following him up the winding oak staircase, you stare at the yellow flame. One of your strongest and most painful memories of childhood returns. It was when _____

_____

_____.

Climbing upward, staring at the light in his hand, you remember another difficult time from childhood. You remember _____

_____

_____

_____.

   Jesus walks past a person standing on the staircase. You stop. It
is someone you feared long ago. It is _____.

CHAPTER 16

A Test

You stare up at the feared one's face and see _____

_____. Just as when you

were a child, you are afraid that _____

_____.

And just as when you were a child, you think it would be best if you

_____

_____

_____.

The feared one says, in a voice you remember too well, "What must you do to overcome your fear of me?"

Summoning all your wisdom, you say, "I must _____

_____

_____."

And then you hurry past, up the winding staircase toward Jesus,

feeling _____

_____.

CHAPTER 17

A Challenge

CATCHING up to Jesus, you want to say to him, "_____

_____," but for the second time you keep silent. Jesus stops at the first landing and turns to you. Set in the oak floor at your feet is a brilliant mosiac. You stare at a golden infant upon a raft of silver reeds in a dark, swirling river.

"Look," Jesus says.

You look at the infant and remember long ago. More than anything else you were a child who _____

_____

_____.

"We will climb higher and you will recall events from the second third of your life," Jesus says gently to you.

You realize this would be from when you were about _____

years old until you were about _____.

Amazed by what has happened in the Tower of Healing, you follow him up the winding stairs toward the second landing. You run your hand over the cool stones of the inner wall, and look upward at the light. You remember important events from the second third of

your life. You vividly recall a difficult time when _____

_____

_____

_____.

Other unhappy images that return to you from the second third of

your life as you climb in the yellow, dancing light are _____

_____

_____

_____

_____.

Ahead, blocking the way, is someone from this third of your life

who caused you pain. You recognize the face of _____.

Jesus walks past this person and you feel the old pain. You hurt

because _____.

The one who hurt you asks, in a voice you will never forget,
"What must you do to be healed?"

"To be healed of the pain you caused me, I must _____

_____," you

say with all your wisdom, and hurry past. But you still feel _____

_____.

Jesus stops at the second landing and holds the torch so that you
can see the mosaic at your feet. It is a white rose rising from a nest
of scarlet flames.

He says, "We are now more than halfway through your life. What
did you do in the first half of your life that you think would be pleasing to me?"

You are surprised for a moment by his question. "Lord, I am not sure. When I look back over my life so far, I am amazed at how quickly the years have passed. When I wonder what I have done that might please you, I must say, _____

_____

_____."

"And what have you done that you are ashamed of?"

"The truth is, Lord, _____

_____

_____

_____."

As you continue climbing the winding oak stairs inside the Tower of Healing behind Jesus and in the light of his torch, you think about the most recent third of your life. You are thinking about events between the year _____ and the present.

You remember a hard time when _____

_____

_____.

Your legs are tired from climbing, but your mind is alive with the past. You remember a difficult time when _____

_____

_____.

Ahead blocking the way is someone you need to forgive. Jesus stops beside _____.

Beneath his torch, the face of the one who needs forgiveness is very clear. You see _____.

"Why won't you forgive me?" this person asks plaintively.

You answer honestly, "_____

_____," and feel _____.

Jesus is silent and you follow him to the final landing.

He stands in a circle of yellow light. The mosaic at your feet shows two snowy peaks beneath a crown of stars.

He asks, "How do you feel about your past thus far?"

"Lord, I see a person who _____

_____

_____

_____."

"What have you done in the last third of your life that you believe would be pleasing to me?" he asks.

You look into his face and say truthfully, "_____

_____

_____

_____."

"And what would be displeasing to me?"

You confess, "_____

_____

_____

_____."

And then you cannot stop talking to Jesus. You have to tell him about all your painful memories. You want to tell him about the scene in the battered wood-framed painting and all the people you have feared and who have caused you pain and who you need to forgive.

You want to open your heart entirely to him about the difficult times in your life, the times of chaos and heartbreak and confusion. You want to leave foolish silence behind. And so you talk to Jesus about your whole past, just as the memories return to you, opening your heart entirely to him.

You begin, "Lord, I must talk to you about . . . "

Talking to
Jesus about Your Past

_____

_____

_____

_____

_____

_____

_____

_____

_____

_____

_____

_____

_____

_____

_____

_____

_____

Talking to Jesus about Your Past

_____

_____

_____

_____

_____

_____

_____

_____

_____

_____

_____

_____

_____

_____

_____

_____

CHAPTER 18

Upon the Tower of Healing

ESUS lifts the iron bar from a door on the third landing and you follow him out onto the battlements of the Tower of Healing. The sun is halfway up the blue arch of the sky. The floor of the battlements is covered with a huge mosaic of a snowy lamb against a violet sky full of comets.

Jesus stands before a wondrous green marble table in the morning light. The legs are carved like four oak trees and curling green marble branches full of fanciful leaves surround the tabletop. Ten gold lanterns sit on top of the table. Five of them hold a leaf of flame.

"Do you know the parable of the wise and the foolish virgins?" asks Jesus.

You look through your Bible until you find the story in Matthew.

"Then the kingdom of heaven shall be compared to ten maidens who took their lamps and went to meet the bridegroom. Five of them were foolish, and five were wise. For when the foolish took their lamps, they took no oil with them; but the wise took flasks of oil with their lamps. As the bridegroom was delayed, they all slumbered and slept. But at midnight there was a cry, 'Behold, the bridegroom! Come out to meet him.' Then all those maidens rose and trimmed their lamps. And the foolish said to the wise, 'Give us some of your oil, for our lamps are going out.' But the wise replied, 'Perhaps there will not be enough for us and for you; go rather to the dealers and buy for yourselves.' And while they went to buy, the bridegroom came, and those who were ready went in with him to the marriage feast; and the door was shut. Afterward the other maidens came also, saying, 'Lord, lord, open to us.' But he replied, 'Truly, I say to you, I do not know you.' Watch therefore, for you know neither the day nor the hour." (Matt. 25:1–13)

When you finish reading, you say to Jesus, "Lord, the way I could apply this parable to my life is _____

_____

_____.

I am like the wise virgins when _____

_____

_____

_____. And I am like the foolish

virgins when _____

_____

_____

_____.

I can see so clearly now, Lord, wise actions lead toward you and foolish actions lead away."

Jesus smiles.

Looking at him in the perfect morning light, you think back over your life and your ascent through the Tower of Healing.

"When I think about my life, Lord, my most foolish actions were

_____

_____

_____

_____

_____.

And my wisest actions were _____

_____

_____

_____

_____

_____."

　　Jesus embraces you. For long moments, within his arms and the perfect morning light you feel _____

_____.

More clearly than you ever have before, you realize _____

_____.

　　Jesus says to you, "It is time to go forward."

CHAPTER 19

Upon the Bridge

mild wind lifts the dark blue banner across the way on the Tower of Blessings and you watch a fold of light move across the white rose.

Christ opens the oak door onto the covered bridge revealing, on the inside of the door, a faded painting of a golden calf.

"Like a fool I have worshiped many wrong things in my life,"

you say to him. "The worst have been _____

_____

_____."

"Then you may enter the Bridge of Ideals," replies Jesus.

You walk out onto the covered bridge with Christ and see it is lined with statues alternating with arched windows. From the first window you can see all the other islands upon the lake. It is bright morning and the frozen lake is brilliant as a silver spoon.

You stand before the first statue and are amazed. It looks exactly like someone you admired as a child. You have no doubt it is a portrait

of _____.

The face is _____. The

whole expression is perfect because _____

_____.

You admired this special person because _____

_____.

As you follow Christ across the bridge, you are stunned to see statues of other people you have admired or idolized during your life. You see schoolmates, adults you have looked up to, and others you have only read or heard about. You see statues of _____

_____

_____.

What many of these people seem to have in common is _____

_____.

When you step out onto the bare, sunny terrace of the Tower of Blessings you cannot wait to speak to Christ. You want to tell him all about these people you have admired and how you feel about them now. Some still seem wonderful, but your feelings about others have changed.

He waits for you.

"Lord, on that bridge I saw almost everyone I have admired in my life. At different times I have wanted to be like each one. The ones

I must tell you about are _____

_____

_____

_____."

Talking to Jesus about
People You Have Admired and about
Your True and False Ideals

_____

_____

_____

_____

_____

_____

_____

_____

_____

_____

_____

_____

_____

_____

_____

_____

_____

_____

Talking to Jesus about
People You Have Admired and about
Your True and False Ideals

_____

_____

_____

_____

_____

_____

_____

_____

_____

_____

_____

_____

_____

_____

_____

_____

_____

CHAPTER 20

Idols and the Ideal

W HEN you have finished talking to Jesus about the people you have admired, you ask, "Lord, what is a good person?" Jesus smiles, opens your Bible, and hands it to you. You read the parable of the good Samaritan aloud.

"A man was going down from Jerusalem to Jericho, and he fell among robbers, who stripped him and beat him, and departed, leaving him half dead. Now by chance a priest was going down that road; and when he saw him he passed by on the other side." (Luke 10:30–31)

You look at Jesus and say sorrowfully, "Someone in my life who

needs my help who I am not helping as I should is _____

_____.

I give no real help to this person because _____

_____.

What I could at least do is _____

_____."

You look out toward the two snowy peaks and wonder for a moment what lies beyond them.

Then you continue reading aloud.

"So likewise a Levite, when he came to the place and saw him, passed by on the other side." (Luke 10:32)

You say sadly to Jesus, "Someone else that needs my help is _____

_____. I offer no help because _____

_____

_____. It would be so

simple for me to _____."
And then you continue:

"But a Samaritan, as he journeyed, came to where he was; and when he saw him, he had compassion, and went to him and bound up his wounds, pouring on oil and wine; then he set him on his own beast and brought him to an inn, and took care of him. And the next day he took out two denarii and gave them to the innkeeper, saying, 'Take care of him; and whatever more you spend, I will repay you when I come back.' " (Luke 10:33–35)

You look at Jesus' kind face and say, "When I wonder, Lord, who of the people I have admired was like the good Samaritan, I must say

_____

_____

_____.

And when I ask myself if I have done anything in my life that was

like the good Samaritan, I must say _____

_____

_____.

The times when I have been least like him were _____

_____

_____

_____

_____."

CHAPTER 21

A Credo

THE sun is a gold coin in a hand of clouds.
  Standing atop the Tower of Blessings, high above the frozen lake, on a clear and pure winter morning, you look at Jesus more intently than you have yet and see _____ _____. You feel _____

_____.

  "I am the Way, the Truth, and the Life," he says directly to you.

  "Lord, _____

_____

_____

_____

_____," you answer with all your heart.

CHAPTER 22

The Tower of Blessings

JESUS stands before the only door on the battlements.

"As you walk down the winding stair inside this tower, you will find wonders," he announces.

You follow Jesus down into the tower. Large windows line the stairwell and no torch is needed.

A huge mosaic covers the entire inner wall and every descending step brings you to a new, brightly colored scene. Every scene is from your life.

You see images of yourself praying, of Christians you have known, of close and loving times between you and people dear to you, of places where you have felt close to God, of events in your life and the lives of others that have been truly miraculous, of churches, of Christ in every form you can ever remember having seen. You see

_____

_____

_____

_____

_____

_____

_____

_____

_____

_____

_____.

Here and there in gold letters are sections you know from the Bible.
There are images of people truly worth your admiration, pictures of
trials in your life you know God has helped you survive, victories you
know God has helped you win. Everything in this mural of blessings
from your life is full of his spirit.

You see _____

_____

_____

_____

_____

_____.

As you emerge from the bottom of the tower into the winter sunlight, you can hardly contain your joy.

"Lord, I have seen all the wonders and blessings you have
brought into my life. I must praise you for . . ."

Giving Thanks to Jesus
for the People and Events in Your Past That Were Touched by His Spirit

_____

_____

_____

_____

_____

_____

_____

_____

_____

_____

_____

_____

_____

_____

_____

_____

_____

_____

Giving Thanks to Jesus
for the People and Events in Your Past That
Were Touched by His Spirit

_____

_____

_____

_____

_____

_____

_____

_____

_____

_____

_____

_____

_____

_____

_____

_____

CHAPTER 23

An Angel upon a Horse

J T is late in the morning and the sun is high and small in the roof
of the sky.

When you have finished talking to Jesus about your experiences inside the Tower of Blessings, he guides you toward the
shore of the island and an archway of red roses. The arch is as weathered and broad as the first, but the path through it is bordered with
two living rose bushes exploding with red buds.

"You began thinking about your past with your sins and ended,
in the Tower of Blessings, with your blessings. Once through this
archway, you will think about your present," Jesus explains.

You remember the first island and the Fortress of Oaks, the Pearl,
the two Dukes of Disorder and the cloak of covetousness. Then you
think about the two towers, the ten lamps, and the Bridge of Ideals.
You remember the sections from the Bible and what Jesus has said to
you.

Looking back over your journey, you say to Jesus as you both
pass through the archway, "Lord, the most important things I have

learned are _____

_____

_____

_____

_____

_____

_____.″

The scent of the closed roses is heavy and sweet. You continue, "Lord,

the greatest blessings in my life were _____

_____

_____

_____

_____.″

Ahead, riding toward you, is a figure in white upon a horse white as sea foam.

"This is the Angel of Faith," Jesus says. "She brings you a difficult task."

You try to wonder what the angel will look like and imagine___

_____

_____.

When she is close enough so you can see her face, you see she carries a bough of cherry blossoms. Her horse has silver hooves. Her gown is white as new snow. She is beautiful the way a cloudless sky is beautiful.

"Tell me, traveller," she says in a voice as sweet sounding as wind upon a harp, "what nourishes faith?"

This does not seem like an easy question. You turn to Jesus, but he wants you to speak for yourself.

"What nourishes faith?" you think. "What do I do that makes my faith stronger? What do I do that makes my faith weaker? I will begin there."

You look up toward the Angel of Faith and say, "What I do in my present life that makes my faith stronger is _____

_____

_____

_____

_____.

And what I do that makes my faith weaker is _____

_____

_____

_____

_____."

The angel puts her hand upon your shoulder and what you feel like doing is _____.

CHAPTER 24

A Testament

As the angel passes, you look at her face against the bright winter sky and see light burning against light.

You follow Jesus across the icy lake toward the third island. You can tell from your pale, short shadow that it is near noon. Ahead a strange figure sits in a boat frozen in the lake.

The figure wears a tall, peaked cap and a tattered gown and sits at the heavy oars as if resting from a hard row. The cap and gown are stitched together from rags that are every color light makes in water.

"This is the Fool of the Lake," Jesus says.

The fool looks up at you and his face is as old and worn as the toe of a boot.

"Give me wisdom!" he pleads.

"If I can," you reply politely.

"Complete the scroll for me. I have no idea what the answers are and feel as if I can go nowhere without them," he says sadly.

He hands you a single sheet of rolled parchment and a goose quill.

You unroll the parchment, look at each unfinished statement, and realize that once completed, the scroll will define your present faith.

"I can only write what I believe," you say to the fool.

"That is better than what I believe, which, at this point, gets me nowhere. I have been rowing since dawn."

You write across the top, "A Testament of My Present Faith." The quill makes letters of gold.

As Jesus watches, you use all your wisdom to slowly complete the parchment.

A Testament of My Present Faith

1. God is _____

_____

_____.

2. The soul is _____

_____

_____.

3. Heaven is _____

_____

_____.

4. Hell is _____

_____

_____.

5. Salvation is _____

_____

_____.

6. Sin is _____

_____

_____.

7. The Second Coming is _____

_____

_____.

8. The Bible is _____

_____

_____.

9. The Church is _____

_____

_____.

10. A good Christian is _____

_____

_____.

When you have finished, Jesus asks you, "Are you a good Christian?"

You answer, "Lord, _____

_____

_____.

You start to hand the scroll back to the fool, but he will not take it.

"I was hoping you would be as lost as I am. A fool only wants foolish company," he says, and doffs his brilliant, ragged cap. "And now I must be on my way." He begins to scrape his oars back and forth across the ice.

Seeing he wishes no further conversation, you fold the scroll, put it inside your Bible, and continue on your journey beside Jesus, think-ing _____

_____

_____

_____.

CHAPTER 25

Blindness and Sight

As you follow Jesus toward the island at the top of the cross of islands, you open the Bible. The sun is almost directly overhead and there is no wind. You are near the middle of your journey. You read in the Bible about two blind men who received sight.

And as they went out of Jericho, a great crowd followed him. And behold, two blind men sitting by the roadside, when they heard that Jesus was passing by, cried out, "Have mercy on us, Son of David!" The crowd rebuked them, telling them to be silent; but they cried out the more, "Lord, have mercy on us, Son of David!" And Jesus stopped and called them, saying, "What do you want me to do for you?" They said to him, "Lord, let our eyes be opened." And Jesus in pity touched their eyes, and immediately they received their sight and followed him. (Matt. 20:29–34)

Watching the one who leads you forward, you ask yourself a wise question about your present life. "What do I do that makes me blind to him?"

You think for a time and then you answer, "More than one thing!

I _____

_____

_____

_____

_____

_____

_____

_____

_____."

CHAPTER 26

Upon the Island at Noon

THE third island on the frozen Lake of the Heart is sandy and studded with boulders as big and smooth as horses lying down.

Walking with Jesus toward the center of the island, you see a circle of ivory pillars. They are standing upon a sandy hilltop among frozen wild grasses. A blackbird with a bead of light in his beak perches for a moment atop one pillar and then flies off to the west.

Climbing the little sandy hill with Jesus, you see a mask hanging from a leather thong upon each pillar.

Jesus says, "These are the masks of love. Look at them carefully and you will know what to do."

He stands in the middle of the circle and watches you.

The ivory pillars are salt white, worn from the weather, standing many times your height, and are arranged around the circle like the numbers on a clock face. Each is carved all over with vines and roses. On the pillar before you, nested high up within a thicket of ivory roses, are two brown swallows.

A porcelain mask faintly tinted with flesh tones hangs from a peg in each pillar.

You start at the pillar that would be twelve o'clock and see, with some amazement, that this mask, like all the others, resembles your face. The cheeks are _____. The chin is

_____. The nose is _____

_____.

You look at your own image and feel _____

_____.

A single word is carved deeply into the base of each pillar. You walk clockwise around the circle, making almost no shadow in the high and small winter sun, and read the following twelve words: *Father, Mother, Brother, Sister, Grandfather, Grandmother, Beloved, Son, Daughter, Relative, Friend, Acquaintance.*

"Here is a mask for every possible important relationship in my life," you say to yourself.

Next you take the mask from the pillar labeled _____

_____. You think about this special person

and feel _____.

The mask is pleasantly heavy and the porcelain skin is cool. You hold it up to your face and look through the eyeholes toward Christ.

And a voice, sweet sounding as a wind stroked harp, whispers in your ear, "What you do that brings the spirit of God into your

relationship with this special person is _____

_____."

With the mask still to your face, you look away from Christ toward the black wall of trees at the border of the lake and the sweet voice whispers, "What you do that keeps the spirit of God out of this re-

lationship is _____

_____."

Looking at Christ once more, you say to him, "Lord, I believe looking through these masks will help me see all the relationships in my present life more clearly."

And so you continue around the circle of pillars, selecting the masks of the relationships that are most important to you. When you look toward Christ you see what you do that brings the spirit of God into the relationship and when you look away you see what keeps the spirit of God out of the relationship.

The masks you choose are: _____

_____

_____.

And What Happens
among the Masks of Love Is . . .

_____

_____

_____

_____

_____

_____

_____

_____

_____

_____

_____

_____

_____

_____

_____

_____

And What Happens among the Masks of Love Is . . .

_____

_____

_____

_____

_____

_____

_____

_____

_____

_____

_____

_____

_____

_____

_____

CHAPTER 27

A Gift

AFTER you have finished looking through the last mask of love, you say to Jesus, "Lord, what I have learned about my present life is _____

_____

_____

_____

_____

_____."

Jesus walks toward you and from the folds of his robe he brings forth a small book. It is no larger than his palm and the cover is a constellation of pearls.

"This is the Book of Visions," he says, and then you wake up.

CHAPTER 28

Awake

T HERE is nothing above you but darkness.

You pull the covers up to your chin and remember the

dream. Most vivid is _____

_____ and _____

_____ and _____

_____.

Your heart whispers to God," _____

_____."

Outside you hear someone shout in the street. A dog barks somewhere. You remember three yellow leaves blowing across the frozen
ground.

There are many things you need to pray about. You need to give
thanks and you need to ask for blessing and you need to seek guid-
ance.

You look up into the shallow darkness above your bed and open
your heart to the Lord, saying . . .

The First Prayer

_____

_____

_____

_____

_____

_____

_____

_____

_____

_____

_____

_____

_____

CHAPTER 29

The Return

You can hear nothing but your own breathing. Sleep will not come. The same worries return to you that often, in your present life, keep you awake. You worry about _____

_____

_____.

"How could these problems bring me closer to God?" you ask, and are surprised at the wisdom of your question.

And you answer, "Perhaps _____

_____

_____

_____."

You see, if only in imagination, the heavy pearl cover of the Book of Visions. Jesus' hand is in a cloud of lights. You can see him opening the book. What is inside?

You need wisdom about many things. Some of the decisions you

are facing are _____

_____

_____.

The greatest problems that plague you are _____

_____

_____.

You turn your heart to God, saying "_____

_____

_____."

Something inside you opens and then you feel God move across your spirit like light upon water. For a long precious moment you feel your spirit filled with God like a lake filled with light.

A dream faintly begins. You row upon a lake at dawn and cannot tell the water from the fiery sheets of dawn light and you put your hand down into the lake and touch something that is neither light nor water. Then the dream continues and the light rises slowly from the water and hangs like a robe of light, a light-filled cloud, in the middle of the air. And then a wintry light is dazzling your eyes and there is a circle of ivory pillars and you see your hand beside the hand of Jesus.

CHAPTER 30

The Greatest Problem

JESUS opens the Book of Visions and the first page glitters for a moment like it is made of sunlight. Then you see the blue engraving of a massive, knotted rope.

The words within an arbor of grapevines across the top of the page are "The Knot at the Center of the Heart." You look up into Jesus' loving face. Around his head is a halo of winter clouds and pearl bright winter sky.

You know _____

_____

_____.

"There are only three pages in the Book of Visions," he says to you. "The fourth page is ahead on our journey."

He hands you the book and you sit together within the circle of ivory pillars.

You stare at the knot and feel a tightness in your own heart.

The rope is as big as your forearm and twisted around like a tangle of black roots or like a snake lost within itself.

Your shoulder touches his shoulder and you feel _____

_____.

The knot at the center of the heart, you realize, is the one problem

in your present life that is the most difficult for you to unravel. It is
the problem you have with _____

_____.

    What you have tried to do to solve this problem is _____

_____

_____.

The most successful solution seemed to be _____

_____

_____

but _____

_____.

You still feel lost within the coils of an endless knot.

    Again, you need to open your heart to Jesus. You want to talk to
him about all the aspects of this knot, how it influences relationships
with others in your present life, what you have tried to do about it,
and why it seems so difficult to unravel. Sitting within the circle of
ivory pillars, you realize finally that this problem is so painful because
it keeps you from loving others more fully.

    You turn to Jesus and say . . .

A Talk with Jesus about
a Major Problem in Your Present Life

_____

_____

_____

_____

_____

_____

_____

_____

_____

_____

_____

_____

_____

_____

_____

_____

_____

_____

_____

A Talk with Jesus about
a Major Problem in Your Present Life

_____

_____

_____

_____

_____

_____

_____

_____

_____

_____

_____

_____

_____

_____

_____

_____

CHAPTER 31

Three Answers

WHEN you have finished Jesus does not reply. He turns to the next page of the Book of Visions for you. The page flashes like light upon a blackbird's wing and then you see a brightly tinted picture of three crosses. The crosses stand in a green glade with two snowy mountains behind them. The words embroidered within a bower of roses and lambs across the top of the page are "The Meadow of Healing."

The colors on the crosses are brilliant as molten glass. The cross on the left is silver, the cross on the right is gold, and the central cross is entwined with roses red as the heart's blood.

Inspiration, like fire around your heart, makes you exclaim, "I am

healed when I _____!

And when I _____!

And when I _____!"

In an intoxication of joy, you turn to the third page and see a face.

The words in a bright hedge of flame across the top of the page are "The Face of God."

The face is _____

_____

_____

_____.

You touch the page with your hand and feel _____

_____.

Jesus says lovingly to you, "If you are heavy burdened, come to me and I will give you rest."

You turn from the book to him and say, "Lord, _____

_____

_____

_____

_____

_____."

CHAPTER 32

Pages of Light

THE sun is past the zenith.

You hand Jesus the Book of Visions and he returns it to his robe. You wonder where ahead you will find the fourth page.

Walking beside him off the island of the masks of love and onto the lake, you open your Bible.

The sun lays a page of light upon each page you turn. You think

of the sections in the Bible that mean the most to you, like _____

_____

_____

_____

_____.

The section that, for some reason, seems to apply best to your

present life is _____.

You turn to it and read the words, "_____

_____

_____

_____

_____

_____."

The wisdom you gain about your present life from this powerful

section is _____

_____

_____.

There is a dove-shaped cloud above the sun. You turn to your

teacher and say, "_____

_____

_____

_____."

CHAPTER 33

A Remembrance

IN the middle distance upon the frozen lake, you see a wagon full of sheaves of wheat. The sheaves are stacked neatly in a yellow pyramid behind the driver. The wagon is pulled by four horses white as lamb's wool.

Jesus says, "This is the Angel of Charity. She brings you a difficult task."

The driver is wearing _____

and you feel _____.

When the angel is near enough to speak to you, the horses halt. Their bridles are hung with silver bells and their manes are white and fine as corn silk.

You squint up into the angel's face. It is like looking at a sun ball in water.

The angel says, "There is nothing clever in my question, traveller. Tell me what you do for the poor."

You think of the people you saw before you began your journey.

You remember a time when _____

_____

_____

_____.

You wonder what you have done for the poor in your present life and answer honestly, "_____

_____

_____

_____."

The angel breaks a stalk of wheat from a golden sheaf and hands it to you. It is delicate in your hand and made of gold wire and finely hammered gold.

She says, "Remember this when you turn away the poor."

"When you turn away those in need you turn away me," Jesus says directly to you.

You answer, "My Lord, _____

_____

_____

_____

_____."

CHAPTER 34

A Discovery

THE fourth island rises high above the lake like a cathedral of stone and oaks. Above the forested stone ramparts of the island is a cliff of fog balanced upon the tops of snowy trees.

You walk beside Jesus toward the fourth island and think how most of the days in your present life follow the same circle.

What you do most mornings is _____

and _____.

And what you are usually thinking about is either _____

or _____or perhaps _____

_____.

Most afternoons find you _____

_____.

A normal evening contains _____

_____

_____.

Your last thoughts at night are often about _____

_____

The creamy fog begins to sink upon the fourth island.

With Jesus at your side, you realize you really only need to answer two questions on your journey.

First, what brings you closer to God? Second, what takes you away from him? You feel as if these two questions, in some sense, are what your whole dream has been about.

You can see close times to him in your past and distant times

from him. One of the closest was when _____

_____

and one of the farthest was when _____

_____

"I have two selves," you say to yourself.

The old self, the one you want to leave behind, has its own values, goals, attitudes, worries, and habits, and all these things take you far from God. The new self, the one you see coming to birth in the brightest parts of your past and that you want to strengthen, has its own life and relationships, and everything it does takes you closer to God. You wonder what you do on a normal day in your present life that gives the old self strength. What do you do that brings the new self to life? You turn to your teacher and confess . . .

Talking to Jesus about
the Old and New Self in Your Past and Present

Talking to Jesus about
the Old and New Self in Your Past and Present

_____

_____

_____

_____

_____

_____

_____

_____

_____

_____

_____

_____

_____

_____

_____

_____

CHAPTER 35

The Stony Mount

THE stony mount on the island ahead is half stone and half fog. It is late in the day and you are shorter than your faint shadow.

You follow Jesus across a rumpled quilt of snow and stones up the shore of the island and begin to climb.

A faint trail winds upward though the wet boulders. The fog is so low you feel you are going to climb through the sky.

Looking back across the lake, you can see your footprints intertwining with those of Jesus. You think _____

_____.

And then you are lost.

CHAPTER 36

Lost

THERE is nothing around you but fog and snowy oaks and hillocks of boulders. You see for a moment a moving shape higher up. You climb and see nothing and then, nothing still. Your heart whispers, "So easily lost!"

You feel exactly like you did when _____

_____

_____.

You give yourself the wisest counsel you can, saying, "_____

_____

_____."

As you try to make your way upward, you think about your present life. The one thing, more than any other, that makes you lose

sight of God is _____

_____.

"And that," you say aloud in the wilderness of snowy oaks and stones and fog, "is what I now remember and keep forgetting."

CHAPTER 37

The One Path

You climb through a castle of fog.

One damp path looks no better than another.

"What will guide me?" you ask. Something wisely answers, "The story of his life."

And so you wander upon the stony mountain inside another mountain of fog, going as much to the right and left as upward, whispering to yourself the story of the only way you have to follow, all you know of Jesus' life.

You say, "He was born . . ."

The Path of Jesus' Life

_____

_____

_____

_____

_____

_____

_____

_____

_____

_____

_____

_____

_____

_____

_____

_____

_____

The Path of Jesus' Life

CHAPTER 38

In the Middle of the Air

JESUS stands before you with the foggy clouds and the stony mountain and all the snowy world at his feet.

He stands outlined against the bright sky with the afternoon sun above his right shoulder.

He says to no one in the world but you:

"Blessed are the poor in spirit, for theirs is the kingdom of heaven.

"Blessed are those who mourn, for they shall be comforted.

"Blessed are the meek, for they shall inherit the earth.

"Blessed are those who hunger and thirst for righteousness, for they shall be satisfied.

"Blessed are the merciful, for they shall obtain mercy.

"Blessed are the pure in heart, for they shall see God.

"Blessed are the peacemakers, for they shall be called sons of God.

"Blessed are those who are persecuted for righteousness' sake, for theirs is the kingdom of heaven.

"Blessed are you when men revile you and persecute you and utter all kinds of evil against you falsely on my account. Rejoice and be glad, for your reward is great in heaven, for so men persecuted the prophets who were before you." (Matt. 5:3–12)

You hear and are silent.

With nothing but the gray fog beneath and the wintry sky overhead, you feel you stand below him in the middle of the air.

CHAPTER 39

Judas

You stand with Jesus upon the foggy mount of the fourth island. He opens the Bible for you and for a moment the sun bright pages are edged with fire.

You follow his finger across the page.

You cannot concentrate. You read scattered phrases through your tears.

Then one of the twelve, who was called Judas Iscariot, went to the chief priests. (Matt. 26:14)

Now as they were eating, Jesus took bread, and blessed, and broke it, and gave it to the disciples and said, "Take, eat; this is my body." (Matt. 26:26)

Then Jesus went with them to a place called Gethsemane, and he said to his disciples, "Sit here, while I go yonder and pray." (Matt. 26:36)

And going a little farther he fell on his face and prayed, "My Father, if it be possible, let this cup pass from me; nevertheless, not as I will, but as thou wilt." (Matt. 26:39)

While he was still speaking, Judas came, one of the twelve, and with him a great crowd with swords and clubs, from the chief priests and the elders of the people. (Matt. 26:47)

Now the betrayer had given them a sign, saying, "The one I shall kiss is the man; seize him." And he came up to Jesus at once and said, "Hail, Master!" And he kissed him. Jesus said to him, "Friend, why are you here?" Then they came up and laid hands on Jesus and seized him. (Matt. 26:48–50)

You look at his face against the sky and see _____

_____.

You ask yourself the most painful question about your present life.

You ask, "How do I betray him? How am I like Judas?"

And you answer, "_____

_____

_____

_____

_____."

CHAPTER 40

The Third Duke

THE descent following Jesus through the maze of boulders and haze is swift.

One question occupies you.

"How can I be his betrayer?"

You think back to your personal testament and your definition of a good Christian and wonder if one more term shouldn't have been defined there.

"A Judas is one who _____

_____

_____."

Just as you are leaving the shore of the fourth island, you see ahead an archway. The arch is as tall as the first two but is covered with sprays of wild, white lilies.

Jesus says, "This is the Arch of the Future. From here onward you will think about the years that remain to you."

As you walk through the arch with Jesus, the fragrance of the lilies fills you with joy. "Oh Lord," you announce, "with your help I

will be _____

_____

_____."

You stay close beside Jesus as you leave the Arch of the Future and begin to walk back toward the island at the foot of the cross. The fog all around is full of light but you can see nothing ahead and only the solid darkness of the mount behind.

You think about your future. "The new self would seek God by

_____

_____

_____

and the old self would wander from God by seeking _____

_____

_____."

Ahead, standing motionless in the fog, is a horseman all in red.

For the first time since the morning you feel cold.

The silk trappings upon the horse and the rider's armor and helmet are red as glowing coals.

You recognize the merry tone of his voice as he greets you, "Traveller! I have been waiting for you and freezing! I am Foolish Worry, the third Merry Duke of Disorder!"

Jesus looks at you.

You say with surprising boldness, "Once I was _____,

and now I am _____,

and I wish to be _____."

The Merry Duke laughs but you do not feel chastened. Before he can speak you say, "Upon this part of my journey I seek wisdom about my future life. And I have had my fill of foolish worries. Whenever I look to the future, I worry about things great and small. The great

things are _____

_____,

and the small things are _____

_____,

and certainly the most foolish are _____

_____."

The Red Duke laughs but it is a small sound like a wooden spoon in a tin cup. He has nothing to say.

"What I will do when filled with foolish worry is _____

_____

_____," you proclaim, and laugh a merry laugh yourself.

Jesus starts forward into the fog and you follow him. As you pass the Red Duke, he hands you a braided circlet of red silk. "Then solve this riddle," he says, and tries to laugh but only coughs.

You slip the red braid upon your left wrist where it fits tightly and then you follow the Lord.

The fog closes around the two of you and you stare at the red braid.

It is as big around as your thumb and is made of twelve smaller braids. Looking closely at one of these you count four very fine braids. Each of these braids seems made of finer and finer braids still.

The braid is joined by a gold clasp shaped like a lion's head.

"This braid is a braid of days, and stands for the time that remains to me," you say with wisdom. You are sad to see how small it is. Looking at the one who walks ahead, you know what you must do

with your future. You must stop _____

and you must immediately start _____

_____.

You hear many horses approaching.

CHAPTER 41

The Angel of Hope

You see ahead of you a gold chariot in a foggy nimbus of golden light; white horses that make the new snow they tread upon look gray; an angel standing in the chariot within a blaze brighter than fire.

You try to look at her face.

"This is the Angel of Hope," Jesus explains.

"Good traveller," she says, "what are the faces of Hope?"

"I turn away from my Lord when I hope for _____

_____

_____. And I am his servant when I hope for _____

_____

_____," you say with new confidence.

Behind the angel a seam in the fog opens as if it were a garment of light slowly pulled apart. You see the Fortress of Oaks. And then, for the second time, you are awake.

CHAPTER 42

The Second Prayer

ALONE with your thoughts, you stare across the bottom of your
bed toward the far wall and see nothing but _____.
You know the dream is nearly over. The only island re-
maining is in the center of the cross. You can almost feel the
tight red braid of days around your left wrist. So much is unfinished
in your life!

The things you still want to accomplish are _____

_____

_____

_____.

And so you open your heart to God, saying . . .

A Prayer to God about Your Future

_____

_____

_____

_____

_____

_____

_____

_____

_____

_____

_____

_____

_____

_____

A Prayer to God about Your Future

_____

_____

_____

_____

_____

_____

_____

_____

_____

_____

_____

_____

_____

_____

_____

_____

_____

_____

CHAPTER 43

The Garden in the
Snowy Mountains

THE world is new and full of spring!

You sit beside Jesus beneath the white sail of a boat sailing upon a lake afire with dawn light.

A blackbird flies ahead toward a green island. The sun rises behind this island and sets the water aflame.

In the distance, like two pyramids beside the rising sun, are the snowy mountains.

All the leaves in the oaks upon the shore are glassy with morning light. The lake is more light than water.

The Lord says, "These are the last moments of your journey. We leave winter behind and sail toward the spring island in the center of the cross. You will find wisdom about your future."

You want to promise him something. "Lord, I will try _____

_____

_____."

You look down into the fiery water at your glittering reflection

and see one who could someday _____

_____.

Jesus reaches into the bottom of the boat and hands you a cross set with five silver mirrors.

"Look and remember," he says.

With the dawn light all around you and the air full of spring, you stare into the five glinting mirrors and feel as if you held the whole Lake of the Heart and your dream journey in your hands.

In the mirror at the foot of the cross you see the Fortress of Oaks

and then a hand holding a glistening Pearl. You feel _____

_____.

In the second mirror you see the two towers and the Bridge of

Ideals and remember _____

_____

_____.

In the mirror at the top of the cross you see the circle of ivory pillars. You want never to forget

_____

_____.

In the fourth mirror you see a cloudy mount and are reminded

_____

_____.

What you have learned more than anything else on your journey

to guide you into the future is _____

_____

_____.

The boat bumps ashore.

The island is grassy and thick with oaks standing in bright constellations of leaves.

Following Jesus onto the shore, you find, like a gift lost among the long grasses, a roll of parchment.

"The last page of the Book of Visions," your heart whispers.

Unrolling it, you read, emblazoned within a cloud of lilies and roses and doves across the top of the page, the words, "The Garden in the Snowy Mountains."

The picture shows a walled garden with fields of heavy snow all around. But within the garden are rows of fruit trees standing among low clouds of wildflowers. Arbors are heavy with purple grapes and red roses and at the center a spring lamb drinks from a free-flowing fountain.

You look at this picture as you stand upon the grassy isle in the center of the Lake of the Heart.

You put your hand in his.

And now you are awake.